THIS REPORT CONTAINS ASSESSMENTS OF COMMODITY AND TRADE ISSUES MADE BY USDA STAFF AND NOT NECESSARILY STATEMENTS OF OFFICIAL U.S. GOVERNMENT POLICY

Voluntary _ Public

Date: 10/26/2015

GAIN Report Number: 2015-1

Dominican Republic

Post: Santo Domingo

Dominican Republic Import Requirements

Report Categories:

Food and Agricultural Import Regulations and Standards - Narrative

Approved By:

Morgan Perkins

Prepared By:

Luis C. González

Report Highlights:

This report details the steps which US exporters must navigate in order to successfully place their product in the Dominican market. It includes information on product and trademark registration, labeling, packaging, pre-authorization of import, and customs clearance. In addition to describing each step, this report describes normal practices in terms of who normally takes responsibility for these procedures and the delays and costs involved in each. In addition, this report identified the underlying legal framework governing importation of food and agricultural items.

General Information:

DOMINICAN REPUBLIC
GENERAL EXPORT GUIDE FOR US COMPANIES
Table of Contents

Glossary of Dominican Institutions involved in regulating Agricultural Trade

Attorney General	*("Procuraduría General de la República" or "PGR")*
Automated System for Customs Management	*("Sistema Integrado de Gestión Aduanera" or "SIGA")*
Chamber of Commerce and Production	*("Cámara de Comercio y Producción")*
Customs Administrator	*("Colector de Aduanas")*
Commission for Agricultural Imports	*("Comisión para las Importaciones Agrícolas")*
Department of Agricultural and Livestock Promotion	*("Departamento de Promoción Agrícola y Ganadera" or "DPGA")*
Department of Animal Health	*("Departamento de Sanidad Animal")*
Department of Plant Protection	*("Departamento de Sanidad Vegetal" or "DSV")*
Development Center and Industrial Competitiveness	*("Centro de Desarrollo y Competitividad Industrial" commonly known as "PROINDUSTRIA")*
Director of the Department of Distinctive Signs	*("Director del Departamento de Signos Distintivos")*
Directorate of Foreign Trade and Administration for International Commercial Agreements	*("Dirección de Comercio Exterior y Administración de Tratados Comerciales Internacionales" or "DICOEX")*
Division of Plant Quarantine	*("División de Cuarentena Vegetal")*
Dominican Institute for Quality	*("Instituto Dominicano para la Calidad (INDOCAL)")*
Dominican Republic-Central America Free Trade Agreement (DR-CAFTA)	*("Tratado de Libre Comercio entre Estados Unidos, Centroamérica y República Dominicana (DR-CAFTA)")*
Exchange Agribusiness of the Dominican Republic	*("Bolsa Agroempresarial de la República Dominicana" or "BARD")*
Free-Sale Certificate	*("Certificado de Libre Venta" or "CLV")*
General Directorate of Customs	*("Dirección General de Aduanas" or "DGA")*
General Directorate of Livestock	*("Dirección General de Ganadería" or "DIGEGA")*
General Directorate of Environmental Health	*("Dirección General de Salud Ambiental" or "DIGESA")*
General Directorate of Drugs, Food and Sanitary Products	*("Dirección General de Medicamentos, Alimentos y Productos Sanitarios or "DIGEMAPS")*
General Directorate of Internal Revenue	*("Dirección General de Impuestos Internos" or "DGII")*
International Health Certificate	*("Certificado Sanitario Internacional")*
Marketing Authorization Approval	*("Registro Sanitario")*
Mercantile Registry Certificate	*("Certificado de Registro Mercantil")*

Ministry of Finance	("*Ministerio de Hacienda*")
Ministry of Public Health and Social Assistance	("*Ministerio de Salud Pública y Asistencia Social*", "*MOH*") or "*MISPAS*")
National Office of Industrial Property	("*Oficina Nacional de la Propiedad Industrial*" or "*ONAPI*")
National Taxpayer Registry	("*Registro Nacional de Contribuyentes*" or "*RNC*")
NORDOM	("*Normas Dominicanas*")
Office of Agricultural Trade Agreements	(*Oficina de Tratados Comerciales Agrícolas*" or "*OTCA*")
Phytosanitary Guidance Letter	("*Guía de No Objeción Fitosanitaria*")
Zoosanitary Guidance Letter	("*Guía de No Objeción Zoosanitaria*")
Sanitary License	("*Licencia Sanitaria*" or "*Permiso Sanitario*")
Selective Consumption Tax	("*Impuesto Selectivo al Consumo*")
Single Customs Declaration Form	("*Formulario de Declaración Única Aduanera*" or "*DUA*")
Value Added Tax	("*Impuesto sobre Transferencia de Bienes Industriales y Servicios*" or "*ITBIS*")

Dominican Legislation governing trade in agricultural products [1]

- Law 4990 dated September 3rd, 1958, regarding Plant Protection.
- Law 4030 dated January 12th, 1955, that Declares of Public Interest the Sanitary Defense of Cattle.
- Law 3489 dated February 14, 1953, on Customs.
- Law 42-01 dated February 21st, 2000, regarding General Health.
- Law 146-00 dated December 27th, 2000, regarding Tariff Reform.
- Law 358-05 dated September 9th, 2005, regarding Protection of Consumers and Users' Rights.
- Presidential Decree No. 705-10 that establishes the Regulations for the Assignment and Administration of the Tariff Quotas granted by the Dominican Republic under the DR-CAFTA.
- Presidential Decree No. 569-12 dated September 11, 2012, regarding the Procedure for Allocation of Tariff Quotas for the Products in the Technical Rectification of List XXIII of the Dominican Republic before the World Trade Organization (WTO).
- Presidential Decree No. 505-99 dated November 24, 1997, regarding the Regulation for the Import of the Agricultural Products in the Technical Rectification of List XXIII of the Dominican Republic before the World Trade Organization (WTO).
- Presidential Decree No. 244-10 dated April 27, 2010, which establishes the Technical Regulations regarding the Maximum Residue Levels of Pesticides in Fruits, Vegetables, and related thereto.
- Presidential Decree 528-01 dated May 14th, 2001, regarding the Rules for the Control of Risks in Food and Beverages.
- Presidential Decree 82-15 dated April 6, 2015, which creates the General Directorate of

Drugs, Food and Sanitary Products.

- Congressional Resolution No. 92-99 dated October 13, 1999, that approves the Technical Rectification of List XXIII of Tariff Concessions of the Dominican Republic before the World Trade Organization (WTO) and orders the Adjudication of said Tariff Concessions through Public Auction.
- Resolution No. 024/2006 dated November 22nd, 2006, given by the Ministry of Agriculture, regarding the Phytosanitary Certificate.
- Resolution No. 84/96 dated September 17, 1996, given by the Ministry of Agriculture ("Ministerio de Agricultura), regarding Fresh Fruit.
- The World Trade Organization (WTO) Agreement on the Application of Sanitary and Phytosanitary Measures (SPS) Agreement.
- NORDOM 53 (3rd Revision), regarding the Labeling for Pre-Packaged Foods.

Exporting to the Dominican Republic, a step-by-step guide

It is recommended that US exporters build a relationship with potential Dominican importers for several reasons: (i) those importers should be well-equipped to discuss key topics such as product feasibility, prices and distribution; (ii) for Marketing Authorization approvals, Dominican law provides that the product label must contain the name and address of the local importer, who is responsible-- along with the manufacturer-- for the quality and purity of the product; (iii) the Phytosanitary and Zoosanitary Guidance Letters and permits must also contain the name and address of the local importer; and, (iv) in order to benefit from tariff quota allocations, these can only be requested by an individual or legal entity residing in the Dominican Republic (local importer).

Nonetheless, US exporters can also establish a branch in the Dominican Republic or incorporate a Dominican company and directly import the goods. Once the incorporation process has been carried out, the US exporter can obtain the corresponding marketing authorization approval, the Phytosanitary or Zoosanitary Guidance Letters and permits.

Key steps in the importation process include:

PRE-EXPORT
Trademark Registration Certificate, granted by the National Office of Industrial Property of the Dominican Republic (ONAPI), when applicable
Obtaining the Marketing Authorization / Phytosanitary or Zoosanitary Guidance Letters and Permits
Certificate of Origin
Product Labeling in compliance with NORDOM 53
Pro-forma invoice
Appointing Customs Agents
PRE-ARRIVAL
Bill of Lading or Airway Bill
Import Declaration
IMPORT CLEARANCE
Payment of Import Taxes
Inspection request to the quarantine office at the port of entry
Quarantine controls (when applicable)
Submission of a copy of the Marketing Authorization / original Phytosanitary or Zoosanitary Guidance Letter
Submission of the Phytosanitary or Zoosanitary permit issued by the Department of Agriculture/Livestock Promotion
Submission of the original invoice
Customs Valuation
Product release

The import process into the Dominican Republic may be divided into three major phases: **pre-export, pre-arrival** and **import clearance**, depending on the product category. To fulfill local requirements, the importer must work alongside the exporter, particularly in the initial phase when the documents for shipment are prepared. Most companies use registered customs agents to comply with clearance formalities, although this may also be done directly by the importer.

Prior to Shipment (Pre-Export)

I. **Process for obtaining a trademark registration before the National Office of Industrial Property (ONAPI).**

The trademark application must contain the following information and be accompanied by applicable documents:

i. Application- one (1) original version and one (1) hard copy of the letter addressed to the Director of the Department of Distinctive Signs, requesting the registration of the trademark in question and indicating the following information: *applicant's name and address; mercantile registry number and national taxpayer number (in case of a Dominican applicant); goods and/or services to be protected pursuant to the International Nice Classification of Goods and Services; and printed versions of the trademark's design (when applicable).*

i. <u>Registration Process:</u> The application process begins with the filing of the trademark application. If the trademark is approved in the evaluation stage by the National Office of Industrial Property (ONAPI, per its Spanish acronym), publication fees must be paid. Afterwards, the trademark is published in the Official Gazette of the ONAPI. From that date, third parties have a forty-five (45) day period in order to register their opposition to the application (since the Dominican Republic complies with the pre-grant opposition system). If no third party contests the application within this period, the registration certificate is issued which is renewable every ten (10) years. This process is generally carried out by the holder of the trademark or by the distributor if the latter has a Power of Attorney for these matters.

i. <u>Timeframe:</u> The trademark registration process takes approximately three (3) to four (4) months.

i. <u>Fees:</u> The official fees involved in obtaining a trademark registration will depend on whether the trademark in question is a text or design application and on the amount of classes that may be requested. A text application under one international class amounts to Five Thousand Seven Hundred and Thirty Five Dominican Pesos (**RD$5,735.00**). These expenses do not include attorney's fees.

Following registration of trademark/brands, US exporters should determine what type of import license is required to ensure product access into the Dominican market.

I. **Marketing Authorization**

The Marketing Authorization or health permit (known in Spanish as "*registro sanitario*") is a permit issued by the **Ministry of Public Health and Social Assistance of the Dominican Republic** (**"MOH"**), through the General Directorate of Drugs, Food and Sanitary Products (**"DIGEMAPS"**), for all imported pre-packaged food and beverage products. It serves as a mechanism for government authorities to guarantee that pre-packaged products and by-products manufactured in or imported to the Dominican Republic meet the minimum sanitary standards and are safe for human consumption, in accordance with the Dominican General Health Law, No. 42-01 (Articles

109 and 129), Presidential Decree 528-01 (Articles 5, 6, 7, 8 and 367) and NORDOM 53. The MOH is also responsible for monitoring and controlling health risks associated with the inappropriate use of additives or toxins, as well as the presence of disease-causing organisms and has consequently established procedures for the issuance, renewal and cancellation of marketing authorizations.

Process for obtaining Marketing Authorization Approval before the Ministry of Public Health and Social Assistance:

The marketing authorization application must contain the following information and be accompanied by specific documents:

i. Application- one (1) original version and one (1) hard copy of the letter addressed to the Minister of Health and Social Assistance of the Dominican Republic, requesting the marketing authorization for the product and indicating the following information: *name and address of the applicant; name of the product; type of product and trademark; name or company name of the manufacturer; location and address of the manufacturer; qualitative and quantitative product formulas; list of ingredients; description of the product's manufacturing process; characteristics of the product's container or package.*

i. Accompanied by- three (3) original samples of the product, in the same presentation (package or container) in which it will be sold in the market (in case of liquids, each sample must contain a minimum of 250mL; in case of solids, each sample must contain a minimum of 250gr); copy of the trademark registration certificate granted by the National Office of Industrial Property; copy of the importer's Industrial Registry Certificate granted by the Development Center and Industrial Competitiveness (PROINDUSTRIA); Free-Sale Certificate issued by the exporting country, duly legalized under the Hague Convention ("Apostille"); copy of the importer's Mercantile Registry Certificate; copy of the importer's sanitary license (granted by the Ministry of Public Health and Social Assistance); and, authorization granted in favor of the legal representative of the product in the country, duly legalized under the Hague Convention ("Apostille").

i. Other- Labeling must comply with the format established in the norm NORDOM 53 (3rd Revision), regarding the Labeling for Pre-Packaged Foods.

i. Registration Process: The application process begins with the filing of the application. Afterwards, the samples provided along with the application are sent by the Ministry of Public Health and Social Assistance to the National Laboratory "Dr. Defilló" or to another authorized laboratory by the Ministry, to run a health analysis on the product. Once the analysis and the application are approved, the Ministry issues a Marketing Authorization Certificate with a registration number. The authorization must be renewed every five (5) years.

Generally, this application is carried out by the legal representative/local distributor of the product in the country, but can also be carried out by the manufacturer. Note that the foreign manufacturer must appoint a local distributor before the application is submitted to the MOH, as explained below.

   i.   <u>Timeframe</u>: The process for obtaining marketing authorization approval may take approximately three (3) months (in general terms, given that there is no timeframe established by law).

   i.   <u>Fees</u>: The official fees involved in obtaining a marketing authorization approval amount to a total of Four Thousand Dominican Pesos (**RD$4,000.00**). A certified check must be made in the name of "Dirección General de Salud Ambiental" for a sum of One Thousand Six Hundred Dominican Pesos (**RD$1,600.00**) and another one must be made in the name of "Ministerio de Salud Pública y Asistencia Social", for the sum of Two Thousand Four Hundred (**RD$2,400.00**) These expenses do not include attorney's fees.

*All ingredients contained in pre-packaged food and beverage items should meet the requirements specified in Decree 528-01, regarding the Rules for the Control of Risks in Food and Beverages.

I.   **Phytosanitary and Zoosanitary Permits**

Meanwhile, oversight of fresh fruits and vegetables, processed vegetables, animal products and by-products, tree nuts, and dairy products is the responsibility of the **Ministry of Agriculture**, through the Department of Plant Protection, the Department of Animal Health of the General Directorate of Livestock, and the Department of Agricultural and Livestock Promotion. The Ministry of Agriculture supervises the health risks associated with diseases of plants and animals as well as their products and by-products, and has responsibility for granting the corresponding import permits.

For these products, importation requires presentation of a formal letter from the Ministry of Agriculture outlining the sanitary/phytosanitary requirements for import of that product. This letter it referred to as the Phyto- of Zoosanitary Guidance Letter. Among the products regulated by the Ministry of Agriculture, "fresh fruits and vegetables, processed vegetables, and tree nuts", require a Phytosanitary Guidance Letter, whereas "poultry, pork, and dairy products" require a Zoosanitary Guidance Letter. There is no specific list of which products need to comply with these requirements, however, regulations stipulate that all products with vegetable, animal and agricultural origins, must request these permits for importation into the Dominican Republic. Depending on the type of product, either the Department of Plant Protection or the Department of Animal Health of the General Directorate of Livestock will issue a Guidance Letter to the importer with the requirements for the importation.

In addition, after the Guidance Letter is prepared, the Department of Agricultural and Livestock Promotion will issue an import authorization, permitting the transaction to occur. For sensitive products, this authorization is generally issued directly by office of the Minister of Agriculture. It is unclear under what legislation this document is required, to which products it applies and under what criteria import authorizations are approved or denied. Once the Authorization is issued, both the Phyto- of Zoosanitary Guidance Letter and the Import Authorization letter will be issued to the importer.

Process for obtaining Phytosanitary and Zoosanitary Guidance Letters from the Ministry of Agriculture:

Exporters should keep in mind that Phyto- of Zoosanitary Guidance Letter are issued only following approval of the Import Authorization, and that both documents are delivered to the importer in one package. In cases where the Import Authorization is not approved, the importer will receive neither document. In the case of sensitive products (e.g. dry beans, rice, potatoes, onions, garlic) the Ministry of Agriculture intermittently controls imports by denying Import Authorization letters. Exporters would be wise to structure contracts to minimize the risk of this eventuality.

Fresh Fruits and Vegetables/Processed Vegetables/Tree Nuts

i. Application: The application is made through a form ("Formulario de Solicitud Guía de No Objeción Fitosanitaria") which must be completed and filed with the Department of Plant Protection, with the following information: name of the importer; address; telephone and fax numbers; goods to be imported; quantity; unit of measurement; port of origin; port of departure; port of entry; use; and transportation. In addition, a written request must be addressed to the Division of Plant Quarantine accompanied by the invoice or pro-forma invoice, certificate of origin, and Phytosanitary or Zoosanitary Certificate issued by the exporting country.

i. Fees: The fees involved in obtaining a Guidance Letter from the Department of Plant Health (Phytosanitary Guidance Letter) amount to Two Hundred Dominican Pesos (**RD$200.00**). After this phase is completed, the Department of Promotion for Agriculture and Livestock will then issue the Phytosanitary permit for a cost of Two Thousand Dominican Pesos (**RD$2,000.00**).

For Animals products and by-products

i. Application is made through a written letter (one original and three hard copies) filed with the General Directorate of Livestock, indicating the following information: name of the importer; address; telephone and fax numbers; goods to be imported; quantity; unit of measurement; country of origin and country of export, port of origin; port of departure; port of entry; use; transportation; value of the goods, animal species with which the product is made. This application must be accompanied by the commercial invoice or pro forma invoice.

i. Once the shipment arrives to the Dominican Republic, it will need to be accompanied by the original International Sanitary Certificate (in Spanish) and the original Certificate of Origin.

i. Accompanied by: The US exporter most work with the local importer in order to obtain the Phytosanitary and Zoosanitary Guidance Letters and Permits. The application must be accompanied by copies of the following documents: invoice or pro forma invoice, certificate of origin, and Phytosanitary or Zoosanitary certificate issued by the exporting country.

i. <u>Registration Process</u>: Prior to loading any shipment, the local importer must request in writing, a permit for the importation of the goods. If there are Phytosanitary o Zoosanitary requirements, a Phytosanitary or Zoosanitary Guidance Letter is issued with the requirements for the importation by the Department of Plant Protection or the General Directorate of Livestock, respectively. (If there are no requirements, the request is sent to the Unit of Pest Risk Analysis. The Unit of Pest Risk Analysis will issue its recommendation. After the Guidance Letter is issued, the Department of Agricultural and Livestock Promotion will issue the permit.

i. <u>Timeframe:</u> The Phytosanitary and Zoosanitary Guidance Letters may take up to two (2) to three (3) days, so long as no level of risk is involved in the importation of the goods in question. The permit issued by the Department of Agricultural and Livestock Promotion may take an additional two (2) to three (3) days as well.

i. <u>Fees:</u> The fees involved in obtaining a Guidance Letter from the Department of Animal Health (Zoosanitary Guidance Letter) amount to Two Thousand Dominican Pesos (**RD$2,000.00**). After this phase is completed, the Department of Promotion for Agriculture and Livestock will then issue the Zoosanitary permit for a cost of Three Thousand Dominican Pesos (**RD$3,000.00**), for poultry products, and Five Thousand Dominican Pesos (**RD$5,000.00**), for pork products.

Tariff Quotas and Concessions Processes in the Dominican Republic

For a number of products — especially politically sensitive products — import quotas exist to control the quantity imported or to provide preferential access terms under the CAFTA-DR agreement. Currently, they are two separate processes to request quotas in the Dominican Republic: (i) Allocation of Tariff Quotas granted to the United States of America, under DR-CAFTA; and (ii) Tariff Quota Allocations process for products listed in the Technical Rectification of List XXIII made by the Dominican Republic under terms of its World Trade Organization (WTO) accession (regulated agricultural products).

I. Tariff Quota Allocations under DR-CAFTA

Any individual or legal entity, residing in the Dominican Republic, with the exception of industry associations or nongovernmental organizations, may request the allocation of tariff rate quotas for the tariff concessions granted to the United States.

i. <u>Tariff Quota Application</u>: Interested parties must submit a written application to the Office of Agricultural Trade Agreements ("OTCA") of the Ministry of Agriculture, to participate in the allocation process for tariff quotas. The OTCA is responsible for the administration of tariff quotas under the DR-CAFTA.

Completion of the DR-CAFTA Tariff Quota Allocation Application Form is required along with the following documents:

- In case of Individuals: *copy of identification card; copy of the National Taxpayer Registry as an individual; description of individual's economic activity; certification issued by the General Director of Customs, which guarantees the import history of the goods requested; information on physical infrastructure (i.e., copy of deed or lease, including additional photos of physical space); current safety certificate or health permit, issued by the General Directorate of Drugs, Foods and Sanitary Products (DIGEMAPS) of the Ministry of Public Health and Social Assistance, certifying the safety conditions for handling the goods requested; and, designated address, phone, mobile and fax for notifications.*

- In case of Legal Entities: *copy of national taxpayer registry; copy of the Mercantile Registry Certificate issued by the competent Chamber of Commerce and Production; certification issued by the General Director of Customs, guaranteeing the import history of the goods requested; copy of the last General Assembly of Shareholders, duly registered by the competent Chamber of Commerce and Production; designation of the representative of the company as its legal representative, duly notarized and legalized by the Attorney General of the Dominican Republic; copy of the identity card of the legal representative of the company; information on infrastructure, (i.e., copy of deed or lease, including additional photos of physical space); current safety certificate or health permit, issued by the General Directorate of Drugs, Foods and Sanitary Products (DIGEMAPS), of the Ministry of Public Health and Social Assistance), certifying the safety conditions for handling the goods requested; and, designated address, phone, mobile and fax for notifications.*

i. <u>Allocation Process</u>: The Commission (composed by the Minister of Agriculture, the Minister of Industry and Commerce, and the General Director of Customs) publishes in at least one national newspaper and on the websites of the Ministry of Agriculture (www.agricultura.gob.do) and the Office of Agricultural Trade Agreements (www.otcasea.gob.do), the information on Tariff Quotas available for the next calendar year, no later than October 1st of each year. The deadline for submitting Tariff Quota applications will be fifteen (15) business days after the date of publication of the Notice of Availability.

The allocation of the volumes of tariff quotas will be based on: historical record of the total imports of agricultural goods carried out by the interested party during the past three (3) consecutive calendar years, preceding the calendar year in which the tariff quota is available; the quantities requested by the interested parties, provided they are commercially viable; and, the quantities available for Traditional Importers and New Importers, in the corresponding calendar year.

The tariff quotas shall be allocated as follows: (a) eighty percent (80%) to Traditional Importers and (b) twenty percent (20%) to New Importers.

After the allocation has been granted and published in a national newspaper by the Commission, the importer must obtain a Phytosanitary Guidance Letter, prepared by the Department of Plant Protection or a Zoosanitary Guidance Letter, prepared by the Department of Animal Health of the General Directorate of Livestock. The corresponding Guidance Letter is then delivered to the Department of Agriculture and Livestock Promotion along with the commercial or pro forma invoice, for issuance of the permit.

I. **Tariff Quota Allocations process for regulated agricultural products and by-products of plant and animal origin, protected by the Technical Rectification of List XXIII made by the Dominican Republic upon accession to the World Trade Organization.**

Under the provisions of Article XXVIII of the General Agreement on Tariffs and Trade (GATT) of 1994, the Dominican Republic made a Technical Rectification of its List XXIII of Tariff Concessions for eight (8) agricultural products; garlic, rice, sugar, chicken meat, onions, beans, powdered milk and corn.

Below, the Assigned Quotas to the Products of the Technical Rectification, as established in Presidential Decree 569-12:

Products of the Technical Rectification				
Products	Headings and Subheadings	Volume T.M.	Basic Tariff %	Non-Quota Tariff %
Rice	10.06	17,810	20	99
Garlic	0703.20	4,500	25	99
Sugar: Refined / Brown	17.01	30,000	20 / 14	85
Chicken Meat	0207.10, 0207.21 and 0207.41	11,500	25	99
Onion	0703.10	3,750	25	97
Beans	0713.31, 0713.32 and 0713.33	18,000	25	89
Milk	0402.10, 0402.21 and 0402.29	32,000	20	56
Corn	10.05	1,091,000	Does Not Apply	Does Not Apply

The Commission for Agricultural Imports publishes an Annual Calendar for the Import of Tariff Quotas of the products listed in the Technical Rectification schedule. These quotas are placed for public auction organized by the Agribusiness Exchange of the Dominican Republic (BARD, per its Spanish acronym). The Commission and the BARD publish, in a national newspaper, the calendar for the import of the tariff quotas and organize the public auction on the set date. After those products have been awarded, the BARD issues an auction certification to be submitted to the General Directorate of Customs, for import clearance. In accordance Article 6, Paragraph VII, of Presidential Decree 505-99 (modified by Presidential Decree 569-12), additional quantities can be placed for auction in a calendar year. That provision states that *"if it is necessary to import any additional volumes beyond auctioned Tariff Quotas (TRQ's), after reviewing the shortfall in domestic production, the Commission shall auction additional volumes required, on the same terms."*

Likewise, after the tariff quotas have been assigned, the importer must obtain a Phytosanitary Guidance Letter, prepared by the Department of Plant Protection or a Zoosanitary Guidance Letter, prepared by the Department of Animal Health of the General Directorate of Livestock. The importer does not have to go through the normal process of obtaining Phytosanitary or Zoosanitary Guidance Letters. The Guidance Letters are then delivered to the Department of

Agriculture and Livestock Promotion along with the commercial or pro forma invoice, for issuance of the import authorization. Depending on the product and if it is pre-packaged, when applicable, the importer must obtain a marketing authorization approval.

I.   Labeling

Labeling must comply with the format established in the norm NORDOM 53 (3rd Revision), regarding the Labeling for Pre-Packaged Foods.

Legislation requires the following information on the product's packaging materials: *name of the product, list of ingredients; net weight; manufacturer and importer's name and address; the importer's industrial registry number (granted by PROINDUSTRIA); marketing authorization number (granted by the Ministry of Public Health and Social Assistance); country of origin; batch identification number; manufacturing date; expiration date; instructions for conservation of the product; and instructions for use.* The text must be in Spanish language; it must be legible and intelligible for consumers, in accordance to Article 38 of Law 358-05 for the Protection of Consumers and Users' Rights. No further specifications are set forth by law, regarding text size.

For alcoholic beverages an additional disclaimer must be included with the following warning: "*El consumo de alcohol perjudica la salud*" (the consumption of alcohol damages the user's health), according to Law 42-01, regarding General Health.

The US exporter should forward a sample of the package to the importer to facilitate label development. For products whose label is not in the Spanish language, an adhesive sticker can be used on the original label, containing all of the required information.

I.   Invoice or Pro Forma Invoice

Before shipment, an invoice or pro forma invoice must be sent to the Dominican importer. This document is needed to obtain the Guidance Letters and permits from the Ministry of Agriculture. Upon arrival of the goods, the importer must have received the original invoice since it will be used to clear the goods and for payment of tariffs, duties and taxes.

I.   Appointing Customs Agents

Most companies use authorized customs agents for handling import clearance, although the importer can also process clearance directly. The customs agent is responsible along with the consignee in managing clearance. The customs agent must be licensed by the Ministry of Finance and endorsed by the General Directorate of Customs.

During Shipment (Pre-Arrival)

I.   Shipping Instructions

Shipping instructions include all details of the cargo and the exporter's requirements for its handling. It contains the information related to the sale and the merchandise's condition upon embarkation, such as the quantity of product, form of payment, transport temperature, packaging, pallets used, among others.

In the Dominican Republic, depending on the product in question, several conditions must be met.

- Shipping containers must be cleaned and disinfected before loading the products for shipment.

- Imported fruits and vegetables must be free of pests or symptoms of diseases, and must not have soil, sawdust or foreign matters, with the exception of mosses, previously disinfected, for its packaging.

- All wood packaging must comply with the International Standard for Phytosanitary Measures (ISPM) No. 15, to reduce the risk of introduction and spread of forest pests and diseases.

- Fruits and vegetables should not be packaged or covered in jute bags.

- Fresh fruits must arrive in refrigerated containers, with temperatures between 0°C (32°F) and 2.20°C (36°F) per Resolution 84/96 of the Ministry of Agriculture.

I. Import Declaration

The importer is required to prepare the Import Declaration through the Automated System for Customs Management (SIGA, per its Spanish acronym). Nonetheless, only companies can present the Import Declaration through the SIGA. Individuals must file directly with the General Directorate of Customs.

The process for import clearance is initiated when the shipping company presents the import cargo manifest. The Import Declaration is presented electronically through the SIGA and the following information must be provided: *goods to be imported, quantity, description, value, tariff code, weight, and must contain attached scanned copies of the documents related to the importation.*

The following documentation must be scanned and uploaded to the SIGA: commercial invoice, bill of lading or airway bill, marketing authorization certificate, Phytosanitary or Zoosanitary Guidance Letters and permits, certificate of origin, custom agent's ID card, auction certificate issued by the BARD (if applicable- for products included in the Technical Rectification), among other documents. The governmental reserves the right to require additional documentation. These will be required in original upon arrival of the goods along with the bill of lading or the airway bill.

To declare the goods through SIGA, the Single Customs Declaration Form (DUA, per its Spanish acronym) must be completed. Both the importer and the customs agent have the authorization in a Token previously supplied by the General Directorate of Customs (DGA, per its Spanish acronym). The Token is an electronic device able to access the DGA's database for the details related to the import declaration in question.

Importers have ten (10) days, counting from the date of arrival of the goods to present the Import Declaration. Failure to do so will result in sanctions for late declaration.

Product Arrival (Import Clearance)

After the import declaration process has been carried out, the consignee can request the physical inspection through the SIGA. This is performed simultaneously with the customs inspection by supplementary control staff, which may include personnel from the Ministry of Agriculture (Divisions of Plant and Animal Protection), or the Ministry of Public Health and Social Assistance, among other competent authorities.

Depending on the products in question, an inspection is performed by personnel from the quarantine office of the port of entry, who will verify documentation and perform a physical inspection of the shipment for possible pests or diseases and to take samples for its remittance to the diagnostics laboratory. (If any suspected pest is common, the goods may be released subject to treatment, depending on the level of infestation. If the pest is of quarantine concern, the goods may be returned to their place of origin, confiscated or incinerated.)

Once the physical inspection has been recorded and verified with the declaration and the original documents (which had been previously scanned), the file is revised by the Technical Department for verification of the tariff codes, value, and compliance with commercial agreements, technical rectification, safeguard measures, and tariff quota allocations, among others. Once the file has been approved and closed, payment can be made and the goods may be cleared.

I.   Payment of Import Duties and Taxes of Goods

The GATT Agreement, 1994, mandates that the customs value must be based as far as possible in the price actually paid or payable, generally indicated in the commercial invoice for the goods being valued. This price is called transaction value and is the primary basis for determining the customs value. If this did not exist, or if the price paid or payable could not be accepted as the basis for valuation, this Agreement provides five (5) other procedures on the faculty of the importer to request reversal of the application of the method for valuation.

To liquidate the goods, it is necessary to take into account several aspects:

- The proper tariff code must be assigned.

- According to the Tax Code of Dominican Republic, Law No. 146-00 and its amendments, the calculation of tax settlement is obtained by subtracting the tariff quota percentage from the CIF value, this amount is called Tariff; afterwards, both quantities (CIF + Tariff) are added, the 18% of ITBIS is applied to its sum. The ITBIS is also collected by Customs for encumbered goods.

- In addition, Selective Tax on Consumption may be applied to certain products, such as alcohol.

Payment can be made via a certified check or administrative check. Payment of duties and taxes must be made out to "Colector de Aduanas" and tariffs for customs services must be made out to "Dirección General de Aduanas". All payments can be paid in any of the local customs offices. However, the person carrying out the payment must be certified to do so by the importer.

Payment can also be made electronically, through the e-banking pages of the following local banks: Banco Popular Dominicano, Citibank, BHD-León and Nova Scotia (Scotiabank). An access pin, administered by the commercial bank, must be obtained.

In case of disputes, parties may refer themselves to the administrative tribunals of the Dominican Republic, or may pursue arbitration.

Standard Documents

On average, US Exporters and local importers will deal with 16 different documents during the import process.

1. Trademark Certificate;
2. Free-Sale Certificate;
3. Manufacturing process diagram;
4. Qualitative and quantitative formulas;
5. Authorizations granted to the local importer or third parties;
6. Product Label;
7. Certificate of Origin;
8. International Health Certificate;
9. Phytosanitary or Zoosanitary Certificate issued by the exporting country;
10. Phytosanitary or Zoosanitary Guidance Letters issued by the Ministry of Agriculture;
11. Phytosanitary or Zoosanitary Permits issued by the Ministry of Agriculture;
12. Commercial Invoice or Pro Forma;
13. Import Declaration;
14. Bill of Lading or Airway Bill;
15. Marketing Authorization Approval; and.
16. Petition for sanitary inspection (for quarantine purposes) and clearance;

Illustrative Requirements for commonly imported products

Schedule A: Fresh Fruits and Vegetables/Processed Vegetables

Phytosanitary requirements for the import of fresh fruit.

The application is made through a form ("Formulario de Solicitud Guía de No Objeción Fitosanitaria") which must be completed and filed before the Department of Plant Protection, with the following information: name of the importer; address; telephone and fax numbers; goods to be imported; quantity; unit of measurement; port of origin; port of departure; port of entry; use; and transportation.

In this regard, the following documentation and conditions must be met:

1. An original Phytosanitary certificate must be obtained from the country of origin.

1. An original Certificate of Origin must also be obtained.

1. The goods must be shipped in refrigerated containers at a temperature of 32-36°F.

1. Fruits must meet 14-day quarantine.

1. Certification that the ship was sanitized and disinfected before the goods were loaded.

1. Certification that the goods have been produced and packaged in areas free of *Ceratis Capitata* (Mediterranean Fruit Fly).

1. Authorization issued by the Department of Promotion for Agriculture and Livestock along with the original Phytosanitary Guidance Letter issued by the Department of Plant Protection must be presented to the inspector of quarantine control at the port of entry.

1. In order to obtain the Guidance Letter before the Department of Plant Protection, government fees amount to Two Hundred Dominican Pesos (**RD$200.00**), and before the Department of Agricultural and Livestock Promotion, government fees amount to Two Thousand Dominican Pesos (**RD$2,000.00**). These expenses do not include legal fees.

Phytosanitary requirements for the import of fresh or processed vegetables.

The application is made through a form ("Formulario de Solicitud Guía de No Objeción Fitosanitaria") which must be completed and filed before the Department of Plant Protection, with the following information: name of the importer; address; telephone and fax numbers; goods to be imported; quantity; unit of measurement; port of origin; port of departure; port of entry; use; and transportation.

In this regard, the following documentation and conditions must be met:

1. Phytosanitary Certificate or Health Certificate issued by the authorities of the country of origin.

1. Certification that the ship was sanitized and disinfected before the goods were loaded.

1. If jute bags are used, these must be new.

1. The goods must be free of pests and soil.

1. The goods must be free of mites, whiteflies and aphids.

1. In case of wood packaging, it must comply with NIMF Resolution No. 15.

1. The goods will be inspected upon arrival into the Dominican territory and examined by the Phytosanitary Diagnostics Laboratory.

1. Authorization issued by the Department of Promotion for Agriculture and Livestock along with the original Phytosanitary Guidance Letter issued by the Department of Plant Protection must be presented to the inspector of quarantine control at the port of entry.

1. In order to obtain the Guidance Letter before the Department of Plant Protection, government fees amount to Two Hundred Dominican Pesos (**RD$200.00**), and before the Department of Agricultural and Livestock Promotion, government fees amount to Two Thousand Dominican Pesos (**RD$2,000.00**). These expenses do not include legal fees.

Schedule B: Poultry and Pork

The application is made through a written letter (one original and three hard copies) filed before the General Directorate of Livestock, indicating the following information: name of the importer; address; telephone and fax numbers; goods to be imported; quantity; unit of measurement; country of origin and country of export, port of origin; port of departure; port of entry; use; transportation; value of the goods, animal species with which the product is made. This application must be accompanied by the commercial invoice or pro forma invoice.

In addition, the following documentation and conditions must be met:

1. The products shall be covered by an International Health Certificate (in Spanish), issued by the Official Authority of Animal Health from the country of origin, stating compliance with the following requirements:

- That they come from poultry born and raised in the exporting country;

- The site of origin of the eggs, remain under official animal health control;

- The site is free of infectious or communicable diseases affecting the species;

- The site of origin of the eggs is located within a 30km radius free of salmonella;

1. The animals, from which the animal products derive from, must be natives of the exporting country or must have remained in it for at least ninety (90) days prior to slaughter and/or export.

1. The goods must contain the expiration date and must be good for consumption for at least six (6)

months.

1. Official certificate of Origin.

1. In the case of meat products, the exporting
   country must also certify that:

- That the meat comes from a slaughterhouse with address and approval number of a
  veterinarian, and if they are cut, with the same conditions;

- The meat and packaging should bring a stamp certifying that they come from animals
  slaughtered in approved slaughterhouses and approved by the official veterinary
  authority;

- Acknowledgment that the meat is fit for human consumption; and,

- That the meat was cut in an accredited establishment under the inspection of the official
  veterinary authorities;

- When the authority considers it necessary, a veterinary commission, designated by the
  General Directorate of Livestock, will visit the country of exportation to recognize the
  epidemiological surveillance system and certify slaughterhouses and / or processing
  plants.

- In order to obtain the Guidance Letter before the Department of Animal Health,
  government fees amount to Two Thousand Dominican Pesos (**RD\$2,000.00**), and before the
  Department of Agricultural and Livestock Promotion, government fees amount to Three
  Thousand Dominican Pesos (**RD\$3,000.00**) for poultry products and Five Thousand
  Dominican Pesos (**RD\$5,000.00**) for pork products. These expenses do not include
  attorney's fees.

Schedule C: Cheese, Yogurt, Breakfast Cereal, Tree Nuts, Wine and Beer, Prepared Foods, Condiments, Sauces, and Snack Foods

Cheese & Yogurt

In the Dominican Republic, the importation of products and by-products considered as pre-packaged foods and beverages, including cheese and yogurt, is regulated by Presidential Decree No. 528-01 which approves the General Regulation for Foods and Beverages Risk Control in the Dominican Republic, dated May 14th, 2001.

The General Directorate of Drugs, Food and Sanitary Products or "DIGEMAPS" (before known as the Department for Foods and Beverages Risk Control) of the Ministry of Health and Social Assistance of the Dominican Republic (*Dirección General de Medicamentos, Alimentos y Productos Sanitarios del Ministerio de Salud Pública y Asistencia Social de la República Dominicana*) is the official body in charge of authorizing the pre-packaged foods and beverages, including cheese and yogurt, that can be imported in the Dominican Republic. It establishes the requirements to request the marketing authorization (or health permit) (*registro sanitario*) for pre-packaged foods and beverages.

This marketing authorization (or health permit) (*registro sanitario*) is a pre-import requirement.

In general terms, the requirements to proceed with the importation of cheese and yogurt are the following:

- The exporter company from the United States should designate a local distributor or company who will serve as the legal representative of the product before the governmental authorities of the Dominican Republic.

- The importer must first request before the Department of Foods and Beverages Risk Control, the marketing authorization (or health permit) (*registro sanitario*) application of the product. Such authorization usually takes around 3 months to be approved.

- In case it is the first time a manufacturing company is going to present a marketing authorization (*registro sanitario*) application, authorities may require proceeding with an *in situ* inspection of the manufacturing plant, even if the plant is not located in the Dominican Republic.

- Once the marketing authorization (*registro sanitario*) application of the product is approved, the importer is able to request the importation of the product.

- When the shipment of product arrives in the country, the customs agents may, at their discretion, proceed to inspect the shipment/container with the products. The marketing authorization (or health permit) (*registro sanitario*) certificate of the product will be required by the customs agents to verify if the product has been authorized by the Ministry of Health.

Marketing authorization (or health permit) (*registro sanitario*) Application Requirements

The following documents shall be submitted along with the application before the Department of Foods and Beverages Risk Control, for the marketing authorization (or health permit) (*registro sanitario*):

1. One (1) original version and one (1) copy of the letter addressed to the Minister of Health and Social Assistance of the Dominican Republic requesting the marketing authorization (or health permit) (*registro sanitario*) application of the product and indicating:

- Name, Address and Phone Number of the Requester;
- Name of the Product;
- Type of Product and Commercial Name;
- Name or Company Name of the Manufacturer;

- Location and Address of the Manufacturer;
- Characteristics of the Container and/or Package.

1. Two (2) Copies of the Mercantile Registry of the Importer;

1. Qualitative and Quantitative Formula of the product;

1. Three (3) original samples of the product, with the same presentation in which it be sold in the market for human consumption;

- For solid products, 200 grams
- For liquid products, 250 milliliters

1. Labeling Format in Accordance to NORDOM 53: Labeling for Pre-Packaged Foods;

1. Legalized Document (Power of Attorney) designating the legal representative of the product in the country.

1. Free Sale Certificate (FSC - "Certificado de Libre Venta"), duly legalized, when the product is imported;

1. Receipt issued by the Ministry of Public Health and Social Assistance. The official frees are Four Thousand Dominican Pesos (**RD$4,000.00**) [2]

Pre-Export Requirements

In first place, the US Exporting Company should obtain a <u>Free Sale Certificate</u> of the product, issued by the Health Authority of the country of origin. This Certificate should certify that the manufacture, sell and consumption of the cheese and yogurt is freely allowed in the country of origin.

The US exporter should designate a local distributor or company, who will serve as importer and legal representative of the products in the Dominican Republic.

Cheese and yogurt must obtain a local <u>marketing authorization (or health permit)</u> (*registro sanitario*), issued by the Ministry of Health and Social Assistance.

<u>**Zoosanitary Permit for Cheese and Yogurts**</u>

In addition to the Marketing Authorization Approval, for cheese and yogurts (dairy products) a Zoosanitary Permit must be obtained before the Ministry of Agriculture given that these products derive from animal origin.

The application is made via written letter (one original and three hard copies) filed before the General Directorate of Livestock, indicating the following information: name of the importer;

address; telephone and fax numbers; goods to be imported; quantity; unit of measurement; country of origin and country of export, port of origin; port of departure; port of entry; use; transportation; value of the goods, animal species with which the product is made. This application must be accompanied by the commercial invoice or pro forma invoice.

In addition, the following documentation and conditions must be met:

1. The goods must be accompanied by an International Health Certificate (in the Spanish language), issued by the Official Authority of the country of origin. The certificate shall contain the name and address of the consignor and the consignee and the number and species of the products to be exported.

1. Technical form (in case of first imports).

1. Original Certificate of Origin.

1. The products and sub-products derived from the animals, should be native of the exporting country or should have remained in the same for at least ninety (90) days prior to its sacrifice and/or export.

1. The products should indicate the expiration date and should not expire soon (for at least 6 months).

1. In order to obtain the Guidance Letter before the Department of Animal Health, government fees amount to Two Thousand Dominican Pesos (**RD$2,000.00**), and before the Department of Agricultural and Livestock Promotion, government fees amount to Two Thousand Dominican Pesos (**RD$2,000.00**). These expenses do not include attorney's fees.

Wine and Beer

In the Dominican Republic, the importation of products and by-products considered as pre-packaged foods and beverages, including wine and beer, is regulated by Presidential Decree No. 528-01 which approves the General Regulation for Foods and Beverages Risk Control in the Dominican Republic, dated May 14th, 2001.

The General Directorate of Drugs, Food and Sanitary Products or "DIGEMAPS" (before known as the Department for Foods and Beverages Risk Control) of the Ministry of Health and Social Assistance of the Dominican Republic (*Dirección General de Medicamentos, Alimentos y Productos Sanitarios del Ministerio de Salud Pública y Asistencia Social de la República Dominicana*) is the official body in charge of authorizing the pre-packaged foods and beverages, including wine and beer, that can be imported in the Dominican Republic. It establishes the requirements to request the marketing authorization (or health permit) (*registro sanitario*) for pre-packaged foods and beverages.

This marketing authorization (or health permit) (*registro sanitario*) is a pre-import requirement.

In general terms, the requirements to proceed with the importation of wine and beer are the following:

- The exporter company from the United States should designate a local distributor or company who will serve as the legal representative of the product before the governmental authorities of the Dominican Republic.

- The importer must first request the marketing authorization (*registro sanitario*) from the Department of Foods and Beverages Risk Control. Such authorization usually takes around 3 months to be approved.

- Once the marketing authorization (*registro sanitario*) application of the product is approved, the importer is able to request the importation of the product.

- When the shipment arrives in country, the customs agents may, at their discretion, proceed to inspect the shipment/container with the products. The marketing authorization (or health permit) (*registro sanitario*) certificate of the product will be required by the customs agents to verify if the product has been authorized by the Ministry of Health.

Marketing authorization (or health permit) (*registro sanitario*) Application Requirements

The following documents shall be submitted along with the application before the Department of Foods and Beverages Risk Control, for the marketing authorization (or health permit) (*registro sanitario*):

1. One (1) original version and one (1) copy of the letter addressed to the Minister of Health and Social Assistance of the Dominican Republic requesting the marketing authorization (or health permit) (*registro sanitario*) application of the product and indicating:

- Name, Address and Phone Number of the Requester;
- Name of the Product;
- Type of Product and Commercial Name;
- Name or Company Name of the Manufacturer;
- Location and Address of the Manufacturer;
- Characteristics of the Container and/or Package.

1. Two (2) Copies of the Mercantile Registry of the Importer;

1. Qualitative and Quantitative Formula of the product;

1. Three (3) original samples of the product, with the same presentation in which it be sold in the market for human consumption;

- For solid products, 200 grams
- For liquid products, 250 milliliters

1. Labeling Format in Accordance to NORDOM 53: Labeling for Pre-Packaged Foods;

1. Legalized Document (Power of Attorney) designating the legal representative of the product in the country.

1. Free Sale Certificate (FSC - "Certificado de Libre Venta"), duly legalized, when the product is imported;

1. Receipt issued by the Ministry of Public Health and Social Assistance. The official frees are Four Thousand Dominican Pesos (**RD$4,000.00**) [3]

For alcoholic beverages, including wine and beer, Law 42-01, General Law of Health, requires labels to declare the following disclaimer: "*El consumo excesivo de alcohol es perjudicial para la salud*" in Spanish ("The excessive consumption of alcohol carries health risks").

Pre-Export Requirements

In first place, the US Exporting Company should obtain a Free Sale Certificate of the product, issued by the Health Authority of the country of origin. This Certificate should certify that the manufacture, sell and consumption of the wine and beer is freely allowed in the country of origin.

The US exporter should designate a local distributor or company, who will serve as importer and legal representative of the products in the Dominican Republic.

Wine and Beer must obtain a local marketing authorization (or health permit) (*registro sanitario*), issued by the Ministry of Health and Social Assistance.

Breakfast Cereal, Condiments and Sauces, Prepared Foods, Snack Foods, and Tree Nuts

In the Dominican Republic, the importation of products and by-products considered as pre-packaged foods and beverages, including breakfast cereal, condiments, sauces, prepared foods, snack foods and tree nuts, is regulated by Presidential Decree No. 528-01 which approves the General Regulation for Foods and Beverages Risk Control in the Dominican Republic, dated May 14th, 2001.

The General Directorate of Drugs, Food and Sanitary Products or "DIGEMAPS" (before known as the Department for Foods and Beverages Risk Control) of the Ministry of Health and Social Assistance of the Dominican Republic (*Dirección General de Medicamentos, Alimentos y Productos Sanitarios del Ministerio de Salud Pública y Asistencia Social de la República Dominicana*) is the official body in charge of authorizing the pre-packaged foods and beverages, including breakfast cereal, condiments, sauces, prepared foods, snack foods and tree nuts, that can be imported in the Dominican Republic. It establishes the requirements to request the marketing authorization (or health permit) (*registro sanitario*) for pre-packaged foods and beverages.

This marketing authorization (or health permit) (*registro sanitario*) is a pre-import requirement.

In general terms, the requirements to proceed with the importation of breakfast cereal, condiments, sauces, prepared foods, snack foods and tree nuts are the following:

- The exporter from the United States should designate a local distributor or company who will serve as the legal representative of the product before the governmental authorities of the Dominican Republic.

- The importer must first request the marketing authorization (*registro sanitario*) from the Department of Foods and Beverages Risk Control. Such authorization usually takes around 3 months to be approved.

- Once the marketing authorization (or health permit) (*registro sanitario*) application of the product is approved, the importer is able to request the importation of the product.

- When the shipment of product arrives to the country, the customs agents may, at their discretion, proceed to inspect the shipment/container with the products. The marketing authorization (or health permit) (*registro sanitario*) certificate of the product will be required by the customs agents to verify if the product has been authorized by the Ministry of Health.

Marketing authorization (or health permit) (*registro sanitario*) Application Requirements

The following documents shall be submitted along with the application before the Department of Foods and Beverages Risk Control, for the marketing authorization (or health permit) (*registro sanitario*):

1. One (1) original version and one (1) copy of the letter addressed to the Minister of Health and Social Assistance of the Dominican Republic requesting the marketing authorization (or health permit) (*registro sanitario*) application of the product and indicating:

- Name, Address and Phone Number of the Requester;
- Name of the Product;
- Type of Product and Commercial Name;
- Name or Company Name of the Manufacturer;
- Location and Address of the Manufacturer;
- Characteristics of the Container and/or Package.

1. Two (2) Copies of the Mercantile Registry of the Importer;

1. Qualitative and Quantitative Formula of the product;

1. Three (3) original samples of the product, with the same presentation in which it be sold in the market for human consumption;

- For solid products, 200 grams
- For liquid products, 250 milliliters

1. Labeling Format in Accordance to NORDOM 53: Labeling for Pre-Packaged Foods;

1. Legalized Document (Power of Attorney) designating the legal representative of the product in the country.

1. Free Sale Certificate (FSC - "Certificado de Libre Venta"), duly legalized, when the product is imported;

1. Receipt issued by the Ministry of Public Health and Social Assistance. The official frees are Four Thousand Dominican Pesos (**RD$4,000.00**) [4]

Pre-Export Requirements

In first place, the US Exporting Company should obtain a <u>Free Sale Certificate</u> of the product, issued by the Health Authority of the country of origin. This Certificate should certify that the manufacture, sell and consumption of the breakfast cereal, condiments, sauces, prepared foods, snack foods and tree nuts is freely allowed in the country of origin.

The US exporter should designate a local distributor or company, who will serve as importer and legal representative of the products in the Dominican Republic.

Breakfast cereal, condiments, sauces, prepared foods, snack foods and tree nuts must obtain a local <u>marketing authorization (or health permit)</u> (*registro sanitario*), issued by the Ministry of Health and Social Assistance.

<u>Phytosanitary Permit for Tree Nuts</u>

Finally, regarding tree nuts, in addition to the Marketing Authorization, a permit must be obtained from the Ministry of Agriculture given that these products derive from plant origin.

The application is made through a form ("Formulario de Solicitud Guía de No Objeción Fitosanitaria") which must be completed and filed before the Department of Plant Protection, with the following information: name of the importer; address; telephone and fax numbers; goods to be imported; quantity; unit of measurement; port of origin; port of departure; port of entry; use; and transportation.

In this regard, the following documentation and conditions must be met:

1. Original Phytosanitary or Health Certificate issued by the authorities of the exporting country.

1. Certification that the ship was sanitized and disinfected before the goods were loaded.

1. Jute bags should not be used for packaging.

1. The goods must be free of plagues and diseases.

1. The goods shall be inspected upon arrival to the Dominican territory and examined by the Phytosanitary Diagnostics Laboratory.

1. In order to obtain a Guidance Letter before the Department of Plant Health, the governmental fees amount to Two Hundred Dominican Pesos (**RD$200.00**) and before the Department for Promotion of Agriculture and Livestock the governmental fees amount to Two Thousand Dominican Pesos (**RD$2,000.00**). These expenses do not include attorney's fees.

Schedule D: Legal Standing of Relevant International Treaties

The importation and commercialization of foods, beverages and agricultural products and by-products is largely regulated by DR-CAFTA, the Codex Alimentarius (CODEX), and the World Trade Organization (WTO).

DR-CAFTA. The DR-CAFTA was duly ratified by the Dominican Congress via Resolution No. 375-05 dated September 6th, 2005, and promulgated by the Dominican Executive Branch of September 9th, 2005. In addition to its provisions, Law No. 424-06 was enacted to adapt Dominican Laws to the requirements already established by DR-CAFTA and ensure the application of the latter treaty in the country.

Codex Alimentarius (CODEX). In order to implement the provisions contained in the Codex Alimentarius, the Dominican Executive Branch promulgated Presidential Decrees 170-01 and 1352-04 which respectively created and ratified the National Committee on the Codex Alimentarius ("*Comité Nacional del Codex Alimentarius (CONCA)*").

Article 127 of the Dominican General Health Law No. 42-01 establishes that the production, manufacturing, storage, importation, commercialization, transportation, manipulation, are subject to the guidelines indicated in said law, the NORDOMs and the Codex Alimentarius.

Moreover, Article 24, paragraph II, of Presidential Decree 528-01 incorporates the Codex

Alimentarius as part of the guidelines that pre-packaged foods and beverages need to follow to regulatory compliance in the Dominican Republic. The aforementioned article indicates *"All foods covered by this Regulation and any other formulations and preparations that can be developed, must comply with the food standards developed by the Codex Alimentarius, adopted or approved by its auxiliary technical committees thereof and approved by the General Directorate of Standards and Quality Systems (DIGENOR)* [today, INDOCAL]*"*.

World Trade Organization (WTO). The Dominican Republic has been a member of the WTO since March 9th, 1995 and a Member of GATT since May 19th, 1950. The Dominican Republic's membership in the WTO was duly approved by Dominican Congress through Resolution 2-95. Since then, the Dominican Republic has committed itself to comply with the standards and procedures that regulate multilateral commerce.

Furthermore, within the Framework of GATT, of 1994, the Dominican Republic presented a Technical Rectification of List XXIII of Tariff Concessions for eight (8) agricultural products considered sensitive to the economy, adopted by Congress through Resolution 92-99.

Schedule E: Legal Differences between Law, Presidential Decrees, Congressional Resolutions, Resolutions and NORDOMs

Differences between Legal Norms in the Dominican Republic

The main differences between legal norms in the Dominican Republic depend on four fundamental aspects: (i) the enacting body, (ii) the regulated content/aspects, (iii) the modification/derogation process, and (iv) their binding character.

In general terms, their hierarchical level is as follows: (1) Constitution; (2) Laws; (3) Presidential Decree; (4) Resolutions; and (5) Norms.

- **Laws**. Laws are enacted by the Dominican Republic's Congress. Laws enacted to regulate matters set forth by Constitution and therefore, categorized as "organic" have a higher ranking than special or general laws. Laws can only be modified or derogated by another law enacted later in time and/or by the Constitution. A Law can also be derogated by a judgment issued by a Court with competence to decide the matter at hand.

- **Presidential Decrees**. Presidential Decrees are enacted by the Executive Branch of the Dominican Republic, the President. In many cases, such pieces are issued in a form of a regulation *("Reglamento")* that will complement a Law, providing the specific aspects for its application; therefore, such regulations are subordinated to the Law. They can be derogated or modified by a subsequent Decree or by a Law.

- **Congressional Resolutions**. Congressional Resolutions are enacted by the Dominican Congress, but has an administrative character. The Congress is entitled to issue a Resolution to set forth a position in regards to a national or international matter. Is does not constitute law itself. It can be modified and derogated by a Law, a Presidential Decrees or by another Congressional Resolution, issued later in time. Congressional Resolutions require the approval of the Executive branch.

- **Resolutions.** Resolutions are enacted by the governmental body that is responsible for applying or overseeing a Law, Presidential Decree or any other legal documents. It serves as a decision to a matter that has not been expressly regulated by law.

- **Standards and Norms.** Standards and Norms are, in addition, enacted by the competent governmental body, as authorized by Law, Presidential Decree or Regulations. It provides, for common and repeated use, rules, guidelines, or characteristics for products or processes to be done before governmental authorities and between private persons or entities.

  - NORDOM's (*"Normas Dominicanas"*), in contrast, do not possess a binding character, in accordance to the Eleventh Transitional Provision of Law No. 166-12 (that creates the Dominican System for Quality (*"Sistema Dominicano para la Calidad"*), and are issued by the Dominican Institute for Quality (*"Instituto Dominicano para la Calidad"*) (INDOCAL), as documents to establish the quality parameters and specifications that products, services and processes would ideally require to meet. Nowadays, NORDOM 53 is the only Norm that possesses a binding character, in accordance to Presidential Decree 528-01.

[1] To see the juridical standing of the relevant international treaties in the area, please refer to Schedule C of this Guide.
[2] Other expenses are to be expected, especially if the interested party wished to accelerate the process by using an authorized private/alternate laboratory for sample analysis.
[3] Other expenses are to be expected, especially if the interested party wished to accelerate the process by using an authorized private/alternate laboratory for sample analysis.
[4] Other expenses are to be expected, especially if the interested party wished to accelerate the process by using an authorized private/alternate laboratory for sample analysis.